The Best 50
BAR SHOTS

Hannah Suhr

BRISTOL PUBLISHING ENTERPRISES
Hayward, California

©2004 Bristol Publishing Enterprises,
2714 McCone Ave.,
Hayward, California 94545.
World rights reserved. No part of this publication may be
reproduced in any form, nor may it be stored in a retrieval
system, transmitted, or otherwise copied for public or private
use without prior written permission from the publisher.

Printed in the United States of America.
ISBN: 1-55867-302-4

Cover design: Frank J. Paredes
Cover photography: John A. Benson
Food stylist: Randy Mon
Illustration: Grant Corley

THE BEST 50 BAR SHOTS

Bar shots are a longstanding social tradition. Whether it's a celebration or a commiseration, they bring people together with an unusual blend of ritualism and rowdiness.

The forms they can take are endless; mixed or straight, flaming or iced, shaken or layered, sweet or savory, there's a shot for any occasion and any taste. Most bar hounds have their favorites, but too often we neglect to branch out and try something new.

The following pages are filled with the best 50 shots you will find anywhere, from old favorites to new trends. Bring an intriguing recipe with you to the bar, whether in your head or written on a matchbook, and gather a group of friends together for a new experience. Bond with old friends or make new ones, but always drink responsibly.

MEASUREMENTS

For this book, the measurements are very simple. Most drinks are measured in fluid ounces (oz.) or parts. If a drink consists of 1 part vodka and 1 part Kahlua, it simply means to use equal amounts vodka and Kahlua; 2 parts vodka, 1 part Kahlua means twice as much vodka as Kahlua.

A shot is usually 1½ to 2 oz. in size, but, especially when mixing your own drinks, there is no need to be bound by this measurement. Many shots in this book run slightly larger than this.

Mixing cocktails is an art, not a science. Try to keep that in mind whenever reading a drink recipe. If you can't get the measurements straight—guess! If you feel a bit more sugar would do it for the drink you're mixing—add some!

JÄGERMEISTER

A bar shot book is incomplete without a salute to the amphetamine-like ruler of all straight shots. The heavy herbal flavor is mellowed when the drink is cold. Jägermeister, meaning hunt master, is a bitter German liqueur. Dating from the 7th century, it is made of a complex blend of 56 herbs, fruits and spices. The label features a stag's head with a cross, because, according to legend, the drink's founder, Hubertas, upon losing his wife, would go into the woods alone to hunt. One day, while hunting, he saw a magnificent stag with a floating cross between its antlers. His vision moved him to change his life: he gave away all his material possessions before founding several monasteries and becoming the patron saint of hunters.

1 shot Jägermeister herb liqueur

Chill thoroughly or shake with ice before shooting.

BULL SHOT

This hyper-masculine shot may sound unbearable, but actually has a savory saltiness that is quite delicious. You may choose to serve this one at room temperature if you're feeling bold.

1½ oz. vodka
1 oz. beef bouillon stock
1 dash Worcestershire sauce
1 dash Tabasco Sauce
1 dash salt
1 dash pepper

Combine ingredients. Shake in a cocktail shaker with ice and pour into a shot glass.

BUTTMEISTER

This frathouse shot is more about the name than anything else, but a well-named shot makes for lasting fun at the bar.

1½ oz. Jägermeister herb liqueur
½ oz. butterscotch schnapps

Combine ingredients. Shake in a cocktail shaker with ice and pour into a shot glass.

THIRSTY SNAIL

The landlord of a pub is just locking up, when there's a ring on the doorbell. He opens the door, and there's a snail sitting there.

"What do you want?" asks the landlord. The snail replies that he wants a drink.

"Go away, we're closed, and we don't serve snails anyway". The snail pleads and pleads with the barman to give it a drink, at which the landlord gets fed up, kicks the snail and slams the door.

Exactly one year later, he's locking up again, and there's a ring at the doorbell. The landlord opens the door, and looks down to see a snail sitting there.

"What do you want?" says the landlord.

"What did you do that for?" says the snail.

THE ANGRY GERMAN

Full of German ingredients, this dark, syrupy shot is an acquired taste but a fiery conversation starter.

1 part amaretto almond-flavored liqueur
1 part blackberry schnapps (Black Haus or other brand)
1 part Jägermeister herb liqueur
2 parts Rose's Lime Juice
1 dash salt

Combine ingredients. Shake in a cocktail shaker with ice and pour into a shot glass.

ANKLE BREAKER

Don't let the sweet-tart deliciousness of this shot fool you: too many of these and you may actually break an ankle.

1 oz. Bacardi 151 or other overproof rum
½ oz. cherry brandy
½ oz. fresh lime juice
1 tsp. sugar syrup, optional

Combine ingredients. Shake in a cocktail shaker with ice and pour into a shot glass.

GOOD SAMARITAN

A man is in a bar and falling off his stool every couple of minutes. He is obviously drunk.

The bartender says to another man in the bar, "Why don't you be a good Samaritan and take him home."

The man takes the drunk out the door and to his car. As they go, the drunk stumbles at least ten times.

They drive along and the drunk points out his house to the man. They stop the car and the drunk stumbles up the steps to his house with the man almost dragging him.

The drunk's wife greets them at the door: "Why, thank you for bringing him home for me—but where's his wheelchair?"

B-69

A more complex version of the famous B-52, this is a dessert shot so delicious you could pour it over ice cream.

1 part Grand Marnier
1 part Kahlua coffee liqueur
1 part Irish cream liqueur (Bailey's or other brand)
1 part amaretto almond-flavored liqueur
1 part vodka

Add ingredients to a shaker with cubed ice. Stir till shaker frosts. Strain into a glass with ice.

LAYERING SHOTS

Learning to layer a shot takes a steady hand, a spoon—preferably a bar spoon—a shot glass and a little practice. A bar spoon is longer and thinner than a teaspoon, with a twisted handle.

When layering a shot, be sure to always pour in order from heaviest to lightest (see table following). The higher the proof, the lighter the liquor since sugar content tends to be higher when alcohol content is lower. The goal is to pour successive ingredients so gently that they don't break the surface tension maintained by the previous ingredient.

- Pour your first ingredient into your shot glass.

- Place a spoon in the glass facing down.

- Pour each successive liquor slowly over the back of the spoon.

- Tip: If your shot still isn't layering well, place it in the refrigerator until the ingredients separate.

LIQUOR GRAVITIES (HEAVIEST TO LIGHTEST)

Both heavy and light cream will float on any of these ingredients.

Name	Gravity	Name	Gravity
Grenadine	1.18	Green crème de menthe	1.12
Crème de cassis	1.18	Strawberry liqueur	1.12
Anisette	1.175	White crème de Menthe	1.12
Crème de almond	1.16	Blue curaçao	1.11
Crème de noyaux	1.165	Galliano	1.11
Coffee liqueur	1.14	Amaretto	1.1
Crème de banane	1.14	Blackberry liqueur	1.1
Crème de cacao	1.14	Blue curaçao	1.1
White crème de cacao	1.14	Apricot liqueur	1.09
Coffee liqueur	1.13	Tia Maria	1.09
Parfait d'amour	1.13	Triple Sec	1.09
Cherry liqueur	1.12	Amaretto di Saranno	1.08

Name	Gravity	Name	Gravity
Drambuie	1.08	Benedictine	1.04
Frangelico	1.08	Brandy	1.04
Orange curaçao	1.08	Cherry liqueur	1.04
Benedictine D.O.M.	1.07	Cointreau	1.04
Campari	1.06	Kummel	1.04
Apricot brandy	1.06	Peach liqueur	1.04
Blackberry brandy	1.06	Peppermint schnapps	1.04
Cherry brandy	1.06	Sloe gin	1.04
Peach brandy	1.06	Green Chartreuse	1.01
Yellow Chartreuse	1.06	Water	1
Midori melon liqueur	1.05	Tuaca	0.98
Rock and Rye	1.05	Southern Comfort	0.97

Use any of these ingredients to create your own layered shots.

CHERRY POPPERS

Coffee and cherry is a surprisingly fantastic combination. The layering takes practice but this one layers very well. It actually looks as good as it tastes.

1 tbs. grenadine
1 oz. Kahlua coffee liqueur
1 oz. Irish cream liqueur (Bailey's or other brand)

Layer carefully using the back of a spoon. Pour grenadine first; then Kahlua; and then Bailey's.

WARNING: Consumption of alcohol may cause you to tell the same boring story over and over again until your friends want to assault you.

THE ANTICHRIST

This shot's tasteless name accurately reflects its crude potency. Everclear is tasteless, odorless and very strong, so proceed with extreme caution.

1 part Everclear grain alcohol
1 part Bacardi 151 or other overproof rum
1 part Absolut Peppar or other pepper-spiced vodka
3 drops Tabasco Sauce, or more to taste

Combine ingredients. Shake in a cocktail shaker with ice and pour into a shot glass.

ALIEN SECRETION

Here's another weird but popular name. Some people see pink elephants when they drink, so why not pink aliens?

1 part vodka
1 part Midori melon liqueur
1 part coconut rum (Malibu or other brand)
1 part pineapple juice

Combine ingredients. Shake in a cocktail shaker with ice and pour into a shot glass.

APPLE PIE

Surprisingly, apple juice renders vodka practically undetectable. This is a great shot around the holidays.

1 part vodka
1 part apple juice
cinnamon to taste

Combine ingredients. Shake in a cocktail shaker with ice and pour into a shot glass.

Sprinkle cinnamon on tongue. Drink the shot; shake your head vigorously until cinnamon dissolves; and swallow.

WARNING: Consumption of alcohol may cause you to thay shings like thish.

CHOCOLATE CAKE

With great style and even better flavor, this shot is a grand finale for any evening out on the town.

1 part Frangelico hazelnut liqueur
1 part crème de cacao
1 part vodka
1 packet sugar

Combine Frangelico and vodka in a cocktail shaker with ice. Pour into a shot glass. Lick a patch of skin (any available, with permission) and sprinkle sugar on it. Lick off sugar and shoot.

DOUBLE BRIT

A double salute to the UK. Made with good quality ingredients this shot is suitable for sipping.

1 part Tanqueray gin
1 part single malt Scotch

Combine ingredients. Shake in a cocktail shaker with ice and pour into a shot glass.

FLAMING SHOTS

No doubt about it, flaming shots are cool. But no matter how cool you think you are, only make one flaming shot at a time and be sure to blow out the flame before shooting.

These shots work best in a dark room. If the room is too bright you may not see the flame, which can lead to singed eyebrows or worse. Do not add liquor to a flaming shot, that's just a very bad idea.

With that said, flaming shots are still really cool, as mentioned above. The higher the proof the better the burn. A 151 rum floater on just about any shot will do the trick. Pour a little 151 and ignite with a lighter (matches tend to be messy). Blow out flame and shoot. A sure attention-getter for the exhibitionist in all of us.

FLAMING DR. PEPPER

A complexly executed shot that really does stand up to its name is always a winner.

1½ oz. amaretto almond-flavored liqueur
½ oz. Bacardi 151 or other overproof rum
6 oz. beer

Fill a shot glass about ¾ full with amaretto and top it off with enough 151 proof rum to be able to burn.

Place the shot glass in another glass and fill the outer glass with beer (right up to the level of the shot glass).

Ignite the liqueur mixture and let it burn for a while. Blow it out and slam it. It tastes just like Dr. Pepper.

CHOCOLATE-COVERED CHERRIES

There aren't many things better than a chocolate-covered cherry and this shot imitates the favorite dessert exquisitely.

1 part Kahlua coffee liqueur
1 part amaretto almond-flavored liqueur
1 part white crème de cacao
1 dash grenadine

Combine ingredients. Shake in a cocktail shaker with ice and pour into a shot glass.

WARNING: Consumption of alcohol is the leading cause of inexplicable rug burn on the forehead.

RED HEADED SLUT

A dive bar favorite, this shot is more black than red and packs a sweet, syrupy punch.

1 part peach schnapps
1 part Jägermeister herb liqueur
1 part cranberry juice

Combine ingredients. Shake in a cocktail shaker with ice and pour into a shot glass.

ADIOS

Yup, adios, enough said.

1 part Kahlua coffee liqueur
1 part tequila

Combine ingredients. Shake in a cocktail shaker with ice and pour into a shot glass.

LEMON DROP JELL-O SHOTS

Make these party favorites in "souffle cups"(small paper cups with rolled edges found in restaurant and bar supply stores) You may also choose to dip the rims of the cups in sugar after the Jell-o has set, for a more authentic Lemon Drop experience.

Lemon Jell-o
water
vodka

Prepare Jell-o as directed, except replace half of the cold water with chilled vodka. Pour into cups and chill.

Jell-o Shot tip: Spray souffle cups with unflavored or lemon flavored cooking spray to allow the shots to slide out of the cups easily.

ALL JACKED UP

The color of this one is a bit off, but between the Jack Daniel's and the sugar content its name really rings true. Try not to do anything too embarrassing.

1 part Jack Daniel's Tennessee Whiskey
1 part sloe gin
1 part melon liqueur
1 part pineapple juice

Combine ingredients. Shake in a cocktail shaker with ice and pour into a shot glass.

BAD HABIT

Simple and delicious, this one may really become a "bad habit".

1 part vodka
1 part peach schnapps

Combine ingredients. Shake in a cocktail shaker with ice and pour into a shot glass.

BRAIN DEAD

A brain walks into a bar and says, "I'll have a pint of beer please."
The barman looks at him and says "Sorry, I can't serve you."
"Why not?" asks the brain.
"You're already out of your head."

BLACK AND BLUE

Blavod (blah-VOD) is a premium quality vodka from the U.K. The only difference from regular vodkas is that it is black. The black color is 100% natural and come from a little-known Burmese herb by the name of Black Catcheu. Like regular vodkas, Blavod has no smell or taste, and even though it is black it will not stain your tongue, teeth, or clothing.

1 part Blavod vodka
1 part blue curaçao

Combine ingredients. Shake in a cocktail shaker with ice and pour into a shot glass.

DOA

Honey, mint, heavy herbs and very high alcohol content make this combination complex and deadly.

Barenjager honey-flavored liqueur
peppermint schnapps (Rumple Minze or other brand)
Jägermeister herb liqueur

Combine ingredients. Shake in a cocktail shaker with ice and pour into a shot glass.

DID YOU HEAR THE ONE ABOUT...?
A rabbi, a priest, and a bishop walk into a bar.
The bartender says, "What is this, some kind of joke?"

MEXICAN JELL-O SHOTS

Make these party favorites in "souffle cups"(small paper cups with rolled edges found in restaurant and bar supply stores). These Jell-o shots are perfect for Cinco de Mayo. Rim with salt after set if desired.

Lime Jell-o
water
tequila

Prepare Jell-o as directed on package, except replace half of the cold water with tequila. Pour into cups and set.

Jell-o Shot tip: Spray souffle cups with unflavored or lemon-flavored cooking spray to allow the shots to slide out of the cups easily.

DEMON DROP

A play on the lemon drop, this one is like a really strong screwdriver.

1 part Everclear (or Bacardi 151 or other overproof rum)
1 part orange juice

Combine ingredients. Shake in a cocktail shaker with ice and pour into a shot glass.

FROM THE HORSE'S MOUTH
A horse walks into a bar.
The bartender says, "Why the long face?"

CHOAD

Any excuse to indulge in Green Chartreuse is a good one. Enjoyed by monks, artists and rock stars, this liquor is truly exceptional. Green Chartreuse is the only liqueur in the world with a completely natural green color. The precise recipe and ingredients are known only to a small group of monks. They are also the only ones who know how to produce the natural green and yellow colors of Chartreuse.

1 part Green Chartreuse
1 part tequila

Shake in a cocktail shaker with ice, pour into a shot glass, slam on the bar and drink in one swift gulp.

DUBLIN DOUBLER

This one will make Irish eyes smile.

1 part Irish whiskey
1 part Irish cream liqueur (Bailey's or other brand)

Combine ingredients. Shake in a cocktail shaker with ice and pour into a shot glass.

CHERRY JELL-O SHOTS

Make these party favorites in "souffle cups" (small paper cups with rolled edges found in restaurant and bar supply stores). This is an extraordinary variation on your average Jell-o shot. Try dropping a maraschino cherry into each cup before the Jell-o sets.

Cherry Jell-o
water
crème de cacao

Prepare Jell-o according to directions on package, except replace ¾ of the cold water with chilled crème de cacao. Pour into cups and set.

Jell-o Shot tip: Spray souffle cups with unflavored or lemon flavored cooking spray to allow the shots to slide out of the cups easily.

FIREBALL

This one is hot, hot, hot. 'Nuff said.

1½ oz. cinnamon schnapps (Firewater or other brand)
few drops Tabasco Sauce

Combine ingredients. Shake in a cocktail shaker with ice, pour into a shot glass, slam on the bar and drink in one swift gulp.

SAY CHEESE!
Two cartons of yogurt walk into a bar. The bartender, who is a tub of cottage cheese, says to them, "We don't serve your kind in here."

One of the yogurt cartons says back to him, "Why not? We're cultured individuals."

STRAWBERRY BOMB

Bombs Away! These shots are too good—so be careful, you may end up bombed.

1 part strawberry schnapps
1 part Everclear (or Bacardi 151 or other overproof rum)

Combine ingredients. Shake in a cocktail shaker with ice, pour into a shot glass, slam on the bar and drink in one swift gulp.

WATERMELON SHOT

This shot is a complex imitation of real watermelon flavor, second only to the real thing.

$\frac{1}{2}$ oz. vodka
$\frac{1}{2}$ oz. amaretto almond-flavored liqueur
$\frac{1}{2}$ oz. Southern Comfort liqueur
1 splash orange juice
1 splash pineapple juice
1 splash grenadine

Combine ingredients. Shake in a cocktail shaker with ice and pour into a shot glass.

CHOCOLATE HONEYBEE

Barenjager is a honey-flavored liqueur based on vodka. The name is German for "bear hunter".

1 part Barenjager honey-flavored liqueur
1 part chocolate liqueur

Combine ingredients. Shake in a cocktail shaker with ice and pour into a shot glass.

MALIBU BARBIE

This uberfeminine shot is a favorite with the girly girls.

1 part coconut rum (Malibu or other brand)
1 part vodka
1 part cranberry juice cocktail
1 part orange juice

Combine ingredients. Shake in a cocktail shaker with ice and pour into a shot glass.

RUM AND COKE JELL-O SHOTS

Who'd have thought, really: these are extraordinary. Make these party favorites in "souffle cups"(small paper cups with rolled edges found in restaurant and bar supply stores).

Cherry Jell-o
water
cola
white rum

Prepare Jell-o as directed on package, except replace hot water with hot cola, and replace cold water with half cold cola and half chilled rum. Pour into cups and set.

Jell-o Shot tip: Spray souffle cups with unflavored or lemon flavored cooking spray to allow the shots to slide out of the cups easily.

SAKE BOMB

A favorite at Japanese restaurants/bars, this one is all performance. Be sure to bang the table rhythmically and chant something asinine as others do these. It's all good fun.

1 shot sake
1 beer

Drop shot of sake into beer, cup and all. Slam on the bar and drink up.

The water was not fit to drink. To make it palatable, we had to add whiskey. By diligent effort, I learned to like it.
—Sir Winston Churchill

PINK GIN SHOOTER

This sophisticated shot can confidently be enjoyed with the most discriminating company.

2 dashes angostura bitters
1½ oz. gin

Rinse a chilled shot glass with angostura bitters and top up with chilled, good quality gin. Plymouth, Tanqueray or Bombay Sapphire will all do admirably.

KAMIKAZE

Ever feel like you're intentionally taking your plane down into a crowd of anxious onlookers? Banzai Kamikaze!

1½ oz. vodka
1 oz. Triple Sec
½ oz. Rose's Lime Juice

Combine ingredients. Shake in a cocktail shaker with ice and pour into a shot glass.

I drink when I have occasion, and sometimes when I have no occasion.
—Cervantes

MELON BALL

A sweet and smooth standby, in all of its acid green glory.

1 part melon liqueur
1 part vodka
1 part pineapple juice

Combine ingredients. Shake in a cocktail shaker with ice and pour into a shot glass.

BLOW JOB

These are fun and delicious, especially when you can get 6 or more people to do them at the same time. Bottoms up!

1½ oz. amaretto almond-flavored liqueur
whipping cream

Pour amaretto into a narrow shot glass and top with whipped cream. Drink in one smooth motion with hands behind your back: you'll need to take the whole shot glass in your mouth to do this.

WHAT YOU WISH FOR...

A guy walks into a bar and sees a man with the smallest head he's ever seen. In fact, the man's head is only about two inches high. So, he sits down next to him and asks, "How is that you have such a small head?"

The man replies, "Well you see, I was stranded on a deserted island and was combing the beach, when I came across an ornate bottle. When I opened it to see what was inside, a beautiful genie appeared and told me that I would be granted three wishes. My first wish was for a luxurious boat to take me home." <poof!>

The man continues, "A large yacht appeared just off shore. Then, for my second wish, I asked to be wealthy, and to want for nothing." <poof!>

The man goes on, "A large pile of gold coins appeared on the deck of the yacht. For my third wish, I asked to make passionate love to the genie. The genie told me that she could not do that, so I asked, 'How about a little head?' <poof!>"

BUTTERY NIPPLE

Intriguing, sweet, creamy and a little dangerous. Don't go through life without tasting one of these.

1 oz. butterscotch schnapps
1/2 oz. Irish cream liqueur (Bailey's or other brand)

Pour schnapps into a shot glass, carefully float Bailey's on top and serve.

Two blondes walk into a bar ....You'd think one of them would have seen it!

LEMON DROP

Try this with a Grand Marnier or flaming 151 floater. These shots are best when made with freshly-squeezed lemon juice.

1 part lemon juice
1 part vodka
1 tsp. sugar

Rim a shot glass with sugar. Drop sugar cube or sugar packet into glass. Shake lemon and vodka with ice; pour over sugar; shoot.

"Work is the curse of the drinking classes."
—Oscar Wilde

CHERRY CHEESECAKE

A stroke of pure genius, I tell you, pure genius. Try one with a stemmed cherry in the glass, then try tying the stem in a knot with your tongue. That's a perfect evening.

3 parts vanilla vodka
1 part grenadine

Combine ingredients. Shake in a cocktail shaker with ice and pour into a shot glass.

FIRE AND ICE

Icy mint and fiery cinnamon compete in this shot of the earth's most primal elements.

1 part cinnamon schnapps (Firewater or other brand)
1 part peppermint schnapps (Rumple Minze or other brand)

Combine ingredients. Shake in a cocktail shaker with ice, pour into a shot glass, slam on the bar and drink in one swift gulp.

Always do sober what you said you'd do drunk. That will teach you to keep your mouth shut.
—Ernest Hemingway

FLAMING JESUS

Not a shot for the godfearing sorts or the weak of heart. But what would those types be doing out at the bars late at night anyway?

1 oz. vodka
½ oz. fresh lime juice
¼ oz. grenadine
1 oz. Bacardi 151 or other overproof rum

Shake in a cocktail shaker with ice, pour into a shot glass, slam on the bar and drink in one swift gulp.

MIND ERASER

Sometimes erasing your mind is a good idea, especially when you behave badly. This one is like medicine for the psyche.

1 part Kahlua coffee liqueur
1 part vodka

Shake in a cocktail shaker with ice, pour into a shot glass, slam on the bar and drink in one swift gulp.

PHYSICS CLASS

A neutron walks into a bar. "I'd like a beer" he says.
The bartender promptly serves up a beer.
"How much will that be?" asks the neutron.
"For you?" replies the bartender, "no charge".

POSH TEQUILA SLAMMER

This is an elegant mixture, but a potentially explosive and fiendishly dangerous pursuit.

1 part tequila
1 part Champagne

Fill a sturdy glass with tequila and champagne. Cover the glass with your hand, slam down on a hard surface, and gulp down the fizzing mixture.

B-52

Amaretto may be substituted with Grand Marnier or Cointreau. This shot is easy and smooth for the bar shot novice.

1 part Kahlua coffee-flavored liqueur
1 part amaretto almond-flavored liqueur
1 part Irish cream liqueur (Bailey's or other brand)

Layer Kahlua, amaretto, and Bailey's, in that order, over the back of a spoon into a shot glass.

A MAN GOES INTO A BAR.....

A man goes into a bar and seats himself on a stool. The bartender looks at him and says, "What'll it be, buddy?"

The man says, "Set me up with five whiskey shots, and make 'em doubles." The bartender does this and watches the man slug one down, then the next, then the next, and so on until all five are gone almost as quickly as they were served. Staring in disbelief, the bartender asks why he's doing all this drinking, and so fast, too.

"You'd drink 'em this fast too, if you had what I have."

The bartender asks, "What do you have, pal?"

The man replies, "I have a dollar."

MIND YOUR BUSINESS

This shot was popularized by a bartender named Phil at the best live music bar in New York's Hamptons, The Stephen Talkhouse. It's quite a kick in the pants. Drinking Red Bull with alcohol has been advised against by health officials, but drinking shots in general isn't the best thing for your health. Always proceed with caution.

1 oz. coconut rum (Malibu or other brand)
¼ oz. pineapple juice
2 dashes grenadine
1 oz. Red Bull energy drink

Combine ingredients. Shake in a cocktail shaker with ice and pour into a shot glass.

CARIBBEAN BLUE JELL-O SHOTS

If you're gonna do a Jell-o shot, why not make it blue, and why not use coconut rum? It's a must do in the summertime. Make these party favorites in "souffle cups"(small paper cups with rolled edges found in restaurant and bar supply stores).

Berry Blue Jell-o
water
coconut rum (Malibu or other brand)

Prepare Jell-o as directed on package, except replace half of the cold water with coconut rum. Pour into cups and set.

Jell-o Shot tip: Spray souffle cups with unflavored or lemon flavored cooking spray to allow the shots to slide out of the cups easily.

CACTUS FLOWER

Wanna be a real cowboy? Here's your chance.

2 oz. tequila
2–6 drops Tabasco Sauce, or more to taste

Add a few drops of Tabasco Sauce to the bottom of a shot glass. If you're brave, go for 10, otherwise somewhere in between 2 and 6 might be sensible. Carefully top the glass up with tequila, trying to avoid mixing up the Tabasco. Drink it down in one, and wait for the flames!

THE PIANIST

A guy called Bill is sitting at the bar. From a box, he pulls out a tiny little piano and a little guy about a foot tall. The little guy sits down and starts playing the piano quite beautifully.

Joe, the fellow on the next bar stool, says, "That's amazing. Where did you get him?"

Bill says, "Well, I got this magic lamp with a genie." So Joe says, "That's great. Could I use it?"

Bill says, "Sure", and hands him the lamp.

Joe rubs the lamp and out comes the genie. He says, "I want a million bucks". Suddenly the room is entirely filled with quacking ducks!

Joe exclaims, "Hey! I asked for a million BUCKS! not DUCKS!" Bill explained "Yes, the genie is a bit deaf. You don't think I really asked for a twelve inch pianist do you"?

BODY SHOT

This is more of a game than a shot. Pick your partner wisely. You may also want to try this procedure with tequila, lime and salt.

1 oz. vodka
1 pkg. (1 tsp.) sugar
wedge of lemon

Using the partner of your choice(!), lick partner's neck to moisten. Pour packet of sugar onto partner's neck. Place wedge of lemon in partner's mouth with skin pointed inward. First lick the sugar from neck, then shoot vodka, and then suck lemon from partner's mouth.

TEQUILA, LIME AND SALT

This is unquestionably the #1 bar shot in existence, hands down, no question about it. Use the best tequila you can afford: there are huge differences in quality and taste between different brands. Tequila which is made from 100 percent blue agave plants will be of high quality, and fairly expensive.

2 oz. tequila
wedge of lime
salt to taste

Pour 1 shot of tequila. Lick your hand in the divot beneath your thumb and forefinger. Shake salt on wet spot. Lick salt, shoot tequila, suck lime wedge and slam down shot glass. Repeat if necessary.

LIQUID COCAINE

This name has been used for many bar shots—this one is pretty classy-tasting.

¼ oz. vodka
¼ oz. amaretto almond-flavored liqueur
¼ oz. Southern Comfort liqueur
¼ oz. Cointreau orange-flavored liqueur
¾ oz. pineapple juice
1 splash lemon-lime soda (7-Up, Sprite or other)

Combine all ingredients. Shake in a cocktail shaker with ice and strain into a shot glass.

CHILLED SOUTHERN COMFORT AND LIME

Remember to chill the Southern Comfort beforehand. Tastes delicious!

$1/2$ oz. freshly squeezed lime juice
1 oz. Southern Comfort liqueur, chilled

Add lime juice to Southern Comfort; stir and enjoy.

AMARETTO SOURS

Amaretto, though it tastes of almonds, is made with apricot pits.

1 oz. amaretto almond-flavored liqueur
1 oz. sour mix

Mix amaretto and sour mix. Pour into shot glass.

24K NIGHTMARE

Don't let the tasty spices and flavors in this one fool you. It may go down smoothly at first, but afterwards you'll feel as if you were breathing fire!

½ oz. Goldschlager cinnamon liqueur
½ oz. Jägermeister herb liqueur
½ oz. peppermint schnapps (Rumple Minze or other brand)
½ oz. Bacardi 151 or other overproof rum

Combine ingredients. Shake in a cocktail shaker with ice and pour into a shot glass. Stir, drink—and shake.

THE BOMB

When the fruity flavors hit the carbonation of the soda—an explosion is sure to ignite!

$1/2$ oz. apple schnapps
$1/2$ oz peach schnapps
$1/2$ oz. banana liqueur
$1/2$ oz. pineapple juice
$1/2$ oz. lemon-lime soda (7-Up, Sprite or other)

Combine ingredients. Shake in a cocktail shaker with ice and strain into a shot glass.

BREATH FRESHENER

This is a tasty solution when you're out of mints at a function. However, it is not recommended to try to fool the breathalyzer!

1 mint leaf
1 part vodka
2 parts white crème de menthe

Place mint leaf in the bottom of the glass and crush with a spoon to release mint flavor. Add vodka first and fill with crème de menthe. Shoot!

DAMNED IF YOU DO

Not quite damned if you don't, but everybody has to live on the dangerous side at least once.

³⁄₄ oz. whiskey
¹⁄₄ oz. red cinnamon schnapps (Hot Damn or other brand)

Pour ingredients into a shot glass. Drink as quickly as possible. Repeat as necessary.

FLYING MONKEY

If you're a banana lover or enjoy seeing flying monkeys—this shot is for you!

1 part Kahlua coffee liqueur
1 part Irish cream liqueur (Bailey's or other brand)
1 part banana liqueur

Layer each ingredient. Start with Kahlua; then Bailey's; finish with banana liqueur. If you have difficulty layering the shot use a teaspoon held upside down and pour over slowly.

OATMEAL COOKIE

The Goldschlager in this yummy shooter can also be substituted with cinnamon schnapps such as Hot Damn for a fierier cookie.

1 part Goldschlager cinnamon liqueur
1 part butterscotch schnapps
1 part Irish cream liqueur (Bailey's or other brand)

Combine ingredients. Shake in a cocktail shaker with ice and strain into a shot glass.

PURPLE HAZE

Just because you'll think you're drinking raspberry soda pop doesn't mean this shot can't do any damage.

1¼ oz. vodka
¾ oz. raspberry liqueur (Chambord or other)
1 splash lemon-lime soda (7-Up, Sprite or other)

Combine ingredients. Shake in a cocktail shaker with ice and strain into a shot glass.

SWEET TARTS

When a shot is so good you can't taste the alcohol is when it's time to worry about how many you've had. This is a classic "slammer."

1 part vodka
1 part orange soda
1 part grape soda

Add all into a shot glass. With your palm over the top of the glass, slam the shot glass on the bar to mix up the ingredients and to give it a fizz. Drink immediately.

AMERICAN DREAM

It's no secret that Americans love chocolate. Try this favorite for a shot you can enjoy the whole way through.

1 part Kahlua coffee-flavored liqueur
1 part amaretto almond-flavored liqueur
1 part Frangelico chocolate-flavored liqueur
1 part dark crème de cacao chocolate-flavored liqueur

Combine ingredients. Shake in a cocktail shaker with ice and strain into a shot glass.

AIRHEAD

The name has nothing to do with the shot: you don't need to be an air-head to relish this recipe.

1½ oz. peach schnapps
fill with cranberry juice

Pour peach schnapps into shot glass. Add chilled cranberry juice to fill.

ALABAMA SLAMMER SHOOTER

Old fashioned whiskey is an acquired taste, so try adding a little sweetness to the bite.

1 part Jack Daniel's Tennessee Whiskey
1 part crème de noyaux fruit liqueur
1 part orange juice
1 part amaretto almond-flavored liqueur

Combine ingredients. Shake in a cocktail shaker with ice and strain into a shot glass.

PURPLE HOOTER SHOOTER

The fun purple color of this drink makes it popular, not to mention the crazy name.

1 part Chambord raspberry liqueur
1 part vodka
1 part sweet and sour mix

Combine ingredients. Shake in a cocktail shaker with ice and strain into a shot glass.

INDEX

Adios 24
Airhead 74
Alabama slammer shooter 75
Alien secretion 16
All jacked up 26
Amaretto 7, 10, 21, 22, 37, 45, 54, 62, 64, 73, 75
Amaretto sours 64
American dream 73
Angry German, the 7
Ankle breaker 8
Antichrist, the 15
Apple schnapps 66
Apple pie 17

B-52 54
B-69 10
Bad habit 27
Banana liqueur 66, 69
Barenjager 29, 38
Beer 21, 41
Black and blue 28
Blackberry schnapps 7
Blow job 45
Blue curaçao 28
Body shot 60

Bomb, the 66
Breath freshener 67
Bull shot 4
Butterscotch schnapps 5, 47, 70
Buttery nipple 47
Buttmeister 5

Crème de cacao 18, 34, 73
Cactus flower 58
Caribbean blue Jell-o shots 57
Chambord 76
Champagne 53
Cherry
    brandy 8
    cheesecake 49
    Jell-o shots 34
    poppers 14
Chilled Southern Comfort and
    lime 63
Choad 32
Chocolate
    cake 18
    -covered cherries 22
    honeybee 38
    liqueur 38
Cinnamon schnapps 35, 50, 68

Coconut rum 16, 39, 56, 57
Cointreau 62
Crème de noyaux 75

Damned if you do 68
Demon drop 31
DOA 29
Double Brit 19
Dublin doubler 33

Everclear 15, 31, 36

Fire and ice 50
Flaming
    Dr. Pepper 21
    Jesus 51
    shots 20
Flying monkey 69
Frangelico 73

Gin 19, 42
Goldschlager 65, 70
Grand Marnier 10
Green Chartreuse 32

Hazelnut 18

Irish cream liqueur 10, 14, 33, 47, 54, 69, 70
Irish whiskey 33

Jack Daniel's Tennessee Whiskey 26, 75
Jägermeister 3, 5, 7, 23, 29, 65
Jell-o shots 25

Kahlua coffee-flavored liqueur 10, 14, 22, 24, 52, 54, 69, 73
Kamikaze 43

Layering shots 11
Lemon drop 48
Lemon drop Jell-o shot 25
Liquid cocaine 62
Liquor gravities 12

Malibu Barbie 39
Measurements 2
Melon liqueur 16, 26, 37, 44
Melon ball 44
Mexican Jell-o shots 30

Mind eraser 52
Mind your business 56

Oatmeal cookie 70
Overproof rum 8, 15, 21, 51, 65

Peach schnapps 23, 27, 66, 74
Pepper-spiced vodka 15
Peppermint schnapps 29, 50, 65
Pink gin shooter 42
Posh tequila slammer 53
Purple haze 71
Purple hooter shooter 76

Raspberry liqueur 71
Red headed slut 23
Rum and coke Jell-o shots 40

Sake bomb 41
Scotch whisky 19
Sloe gin 26
Southern Comfort liqueur 37, 62, 63
Strawberry bomb 36
Sweet tarts 72

Tequila 24, 30, 32, 53, 58, 61
Tequila, lime and salt 61
Triple Sec 43
24k nightmare 65

Vanilla vodka 49
Vodka 4, 10, 16, 17, 18, 25, 27, 28, 37, 39, 43, 44, 48, 51, 52, 60, 62, 67, 71, 72, 76

Watermelon shot 37
Whiskey 68
White crème de cacao 22
White crème de menthe 67
White rum 40

THE BEST 50 BAR SHOTS